When the Trumpet Is Blown

When the Trumpet Is Blown

QURAISHIYAH DURBARRY

RESOURCE *Publications* · Eugene, Oregon

WHEN THE TRUMPET IS BLOWN

Resource Publications
An Imprint of Wipf and Stock Publishers
199 W. 8th Ave., Suite 3
Eugene, OR 97401

www.wipfandstock.com

PAPERBACK ISBN: 978-1-6667-7821-2
HARDCOVER ISBN: 978-1-6667-7822-9
EBOOK ISBN: 978-1-6667-7823-6

07/06/23

My dear Artémise,
I write this, as many other lines,
For you
For I believe that my verses
Are all from you.

The fourth angel blew his trumpet,
and a third of the sun was struck,
and a third of the moon,
and a third of the stars,
so that a third of their light might be darkened,
and a third of the day might be kept from shining,
and likewise a third of the night.

—Rev 8:12

1.

In the depth
Of the blue ocean
My love now lies
In the bosom
Of comforting waves
That slowly sway
Her cradle
And lull her sleep eternal

In the lighted depths
Where I hope
The water is warm
She lies in a bag
Cause I could not find her
A well-adorned coffin
I loved her so
But still wanted to get rid
Of the body
That showed no life
And curdled her eyes

In her watery coffin
My baby is safe

I tell myself
From gnawing teeth
And clawing gnarls
How would I have lived knowing
In the soil muddy
My heart was buried
And now lived
In the depth of
A dark pitted earth

But my heart is serene
I built no pyramids
But threw her in the
Foaming tongues
Of the stormy sea
But to heaven same
She must have flown

The only thing I dread
Is the saying
That the sea ultimately throws
Out everything
And sometimes I regret
Missing my baby so much
For fear of wanting her back

2.

That point
Around which everything revolves
Or which revolves everything
A moment, an instant
Of peace
Of pure bliss
As namby-pamby
As that might sound
That little piece of space and time
Flutters
And dies
In a day, a year,
Half a second
A fleeting memory
Convincing you it has been worth
While
Cause nothing before
Is anymore
And nothing after
Matters
Which if one was sure
To get it back
In an afterlife

Would embrace death immediately
And suffer all hellish vicissitudes
That point that always happens too fast
Goes away too early
And which we never realise
While living it

3.

It all adds to nothing in the end
Like o plus o
Or o multiplied by anything
In the end you are still left
With life
And from whatever end you see it
Apart from a slow decaying
Decrepitude
It falls to nothing
I marveled at the blue sky
Spotted with pink
Flamingos
An alluring lure
And you say
One moment more
Until the sky breaks black
And the flamingos fall grey
I see changes and deaths
And from all this rottenness
Comes a shrug
That sees things as they are
And says it was not worth it

4.

I wait
In the melting of candles
And the burning
Of nights
You'll come back to me
From hell or heaven
Or from the depths
Of nothingness
If space itself is matter
Then there must be something
That matters
And if it is not love
Then nothing does

5.

An amalgam of debris
Piles up in the container
A broken rusted arrow
That corrodes everything
Be it worthless zircons
Or gold once white
And yellows olivine
That brings life
No more
A handful of dust
Walls the papery sides
And clogs
Any residual beating breaths
That want in
Or out
And a pit
With a rotting core
Like a forbidden almond
Grows rancid
With time
What's surprising is
That with all these garbage
In its bowels
My heart pumps still

6.

What when a heaven is tattered
And when the silken drapes
You painted your future on
Gape at you with
Wide-eyed embers
When the goal you were running to
Has been removed
But you have to run on
When dreams lie shredded
But you dream on
After you forced shut down
Your lids
What when you built nothing more
Than a towering jenga
And for every 3 blocks you've been adding
One is removed
And what when it all collapses
And you build on and build again
And mend the shreds
And sew the holes
But that heaven will never be
Even with a hole in your head
Or a stake through your heart

7.

The hand that writ

I took the pen
I wrote
I was meant too
Somewhere thousands of years before
Or millions of years
After
If time is not linear after all
Someone
Some thing
A flutter of wings
Or a passing of feces
Decided I'll take the pen now
And I'll write
Determined each word, and letter and alphabet
Don't leave out punctuations
It was all written out
Before being written by me
That's what I say, that what I physically
And philosophically conceive
When I'm having a blue bout
Because I can then flutter about

Without a wrinkle
Without dark circles
Or white hair
I can go without washing my hands
And dream of pastures green
And a heavenly repose
Because the dagger in my hand
Was planted there
Your Honor
And I was framed by the theory
Of chaos

8.

I dream of a world
Running like dust through my fingers
Of people and their towers
Washed away
Like a burrow
Built on a riverbank
Of the sea burning
Of volcanoes drowning
Cities and roads and lakes
And of the sun
Drawn by childish fingers
Smiling through yellow wax
With spikes coming all round its head
Melting
That all things conceited,
And ugly and petty
That is all things human
And all human
Struck down
And the aliens that gave birth to us
Laugh because they are just so fed up
With teeny, tiny, puny us
And from their laboratory bring forth

The mighty dinos
On one side there is the world
And the other you
And my choice was made since
You first looked at me

9.

The door I bang on
Is invisible
My voice rang in the
Void
And your name dies on my lips
Every time I call it
Though I do everything right
I bind my mind
In blind faith
And chant your name
A hundred times
Breaching on heresy
Yet. . .
Your voice does not come to my ear
Not even blurry lines
In the wasteland of my amnesic
Memory
I hold your cloth
Like a talisman to my heart
But my imagination
Fickle as fire in a gale
Cannot fly heavenly high
It wanders about and sets

On the lowly grind
On a dirty, ugly, daily
Regime
And I bang on
From one o'clock to 2 o'clock
As a remembrance of a remembrance

10.

The cradle went this way
And that
Back and forth
And forth
And back
A motion that will die in time
But not now
Not soon
It cradles physics
And mass and matter
It cradles beings I guess
And souls too
I imagine a soul back and forth
Love back and forth
Sadness back and forth
And perhaps petty happiness too
And I imagine a ripple in the future
When you died
And a tear in the past
A thousand years before
Ripping the present
To a cut in the future
Travelling back

And creating the deluge
That drowned all but Noah's Ark

11.

I wish I were made of glass
Beautiful ethereal transparent
Glass
And not this lump
Of solid flaccid meat
I wish a finger could ran on me
And not get stuck
On flabby skin
And crow's feet
Or wrinkles, pimples
And acnes
I wish I could break in pieces
And lie in a heap
Literally
And not just feeling so
Helplessly sealed
In this
Bulging ball of blood and sweat
That never breaks
Apart

12.

I drift about
A wreck of myself
Tattered here
Holed there
Floating the shadow
Of a sail
Too dejected to
Drown or to
Sink
I have been cursed
With life
A torn and patched up
Life
With cloth of colors
So different that it mimics
Easily a blind happiness
A drowsy peace of mind
Numb with tiredness
That wants a stop
That calls for a break
But goes on
Because it has wheels for legs

13.

I breathe a cadaver
Nauseous nought
But me
I live a cadaver
Stiffly pacing
In a similar coffin
Only bigger
10 by 10
Instead of 2 by 1
But it's not a big difference
Really
When you throw away
The clothes you changed
After weeks
Because it smelled
Worse than a rotten shroud
When you change clothes
Faute de mieux
Cause it's not the worst smelling part of you
But only the most easily
Changeable
Or throwable
No knocking, never a hi, and no more byes

The burnt lights and perpetually drawn curtains
Bury me deeper than
6 feet of darkness
The corpse in my attic is me
The one buried alive
Behind walls
Is none but me
And the one rotting
In body and mind
Is also me
The peels of my soul
And my skin
Together disintegrate
And make an only heap
And I still wait for a miracle

14.

I hear the sun shining
And rising of the birds
Things go about merrily
Without me
And I thought of shedding my sorrow
Too
I waited naked
And stripped
Of skin
But nothing grew
Back
So happiness I had none
But forsook my sorrow too
And now bare
And literally in the raw
I have nothing to raise me
Higher than the pangs
Of the flesh

15.

I stagger dizzily at the brink
Of emptiness
But held onto dear
Life
Till you came back
But I was by then
So used to living
Without you
That I forgot all about you
And went on with
Dear life
Chatting and partying
Clubbing as one say now
And then I vaguely remembered
You are back
And I went running and looking for you
And in a closet found you
Frozen hungry thirsty
But I looked on
Because you were back earlier too
And I forgot too
And I knew in all
The little crevices and crevasses

Of my house
There are forgotten yous
Hanging about

16.

When death knocked at my door
The cunt had a smile on her face
And I let her in
Thinking like the clever guy in the tale
I'll outwit the shit out of her
Yea, come on
I'll trick you into giving me
Some more time
I explained choices
Hung crimes on the back
Of a fucked-up psychology
And wicked parents
Painted me so white
That I shone transparent
But death was wily
Wilier than life
And while I cheered to an almost
Won and done game
The son of a bitch
Went through the closed door
Where in the cradle
My baby lay

17.

A life without sound
Lays desert
On the brink
Of a death
Wish
That never comes
And goes on blindly
About
Without cane
Or dog
Fumbling but not falling
Tired of failing
But still insisting
Of perpetuating
Its failing pattern
Like a peel
Without the fruit
It hangs there
Still not falling
Through its rottenness
Its emptiness
Life finds a way
On the pretense

That it is sacred
And can only lie in wait

18.

Miles away
The butterfly fluttered
And the skies drew darker
It flapped again
And there laid
Your body
In my hands
It couldn't stop
And the flowers died
It quivered fleetingly
And still
The chicks
Liquefied into yolks
It will die soon
One hopes
But a last
Flicker
Was all that was needed
To dissolve
Reality into remembrance

19.

The rosary ran red
Between used fingers
Imploring a dead god
Or a deaf one
Little difference there
For the plaintiff
Where dreams shatter
Easier than glasses
Making a prayer is just as futile
As throwing a coin in a pond
And still with a heart
Going brown and rancid
We kneel and scorch our knees
Hoping
And our knuckles go white
Squeezing the coin we kept
For the wishing pond

20.

There must be a way
A way to turn back
We can go to the starting page
Of every book
We can rifle through our writings
And change the chapters
And change the endings
Why is life then such a bitch
That we cannot go back
That we cannot flip through it
Nor change it
There must be a way
A way to the beginning
A way to bring you back
A way for another moment

21.

There are times
When your heart has given away
And feels just like shredded debris
Pulsing in a silent wind
There are times when the grey waves
Of sadness pull over you
And threaten to drown you
There are times when the nothingness
Of matter sweeps over
These are times when the lure of the prayer
Pulls you down
And the scorches on your knees seem like
The signature of salvation
These are times when your hands frantically join themselves
To your mouth
And nothing stops them
Neither your nails burning in your wrists
Nor the peeling of dried-up lips
Muttering prayers from unknown religions
Pain on the contrary triggers you
And someone flogging your back bloody
And pulling you by the hair
In gravel and mud

Becomes a friend
These are times when you are pulled in by faith
And believe the miracle will be
These are times. . .
At others, I'm a staunched atheist

22.

Take me back
Take me back to a time
Where I understood
The song of birds
In the sunny dew
Take me back

Take me back to a time
Where the starry sky
Was a mystery canopy
For a thousand worlds
Lit by camping lanterns
And where we told stories
About dragons, and fairies and trolls
And talking animals

Take me back to a time
Where living and loving
Went together

Take me to that time
Where I yawned lazily
At the rising sun
Where mornings still meant

A new day
With so much to do
Even if they were the same things
I do
Before and again

Back to that time
When a heart was full
And not as greying as my head
Take me back when my stomach
Did not grow a pit inside
Where I stretched my arms
To fly
Where seraphs sung
And mourned not
And the bell chimed
And tolled not

Take me back to that time
When adorned on my lips
Was something else
Than a ghost smile
Reminding me of a time
That was

A time where flying leaves meant
Red season and not dead season
Back when there was time
Time to look far
To the horizon
At the beauty of a creation

And not contemplate
The decaying of it all
And how and when it will all end
Take me back

Take me back to the time
When you were here
Where you were with me
And tomorrow meant a day more with you
A time when innocence and beauty
Still had a meaning

And when I squinted
At the silvery cover of the
Sparkling sea
Ignorant of its
Depth

Spit her back to me
Or take me in
I murmured one last time
Before throwing over me
The blue-green sheet
Of a crashing wave
Covering head, toe and mouth
And gurgled my way
To the bottom

23.

How would you die?

How would you die, Quraishiyah

With a gun to your temple
Or in your mouth
Your head in an oven
Sounds easy but greasy
You don't want soot all over your pretty face

If you could pay someone
To click a trigger at the back of your head
Blowing your brain
Is kind of a fantasy
Or an axe hanging from
Your skull
In a sordid gore tableau

If only you could find a guillotine
Or have someone decapitate you
Preferably in front of a public
You could have been martyr,
Queen or whore

A rope is too much of a hassle if you ask me
And too trivial for a poetic mind

You could burn down with a monument
A golden temple as some romantic
If every goddamn thing were not brick
And unburnable nowadays

What do you choose Quraishiyah,
When time is going so slow
That you have time
To invent a 1000 more ways to die
You could fill a questionnaire,
File a multiple choice with choices running
From A to Z
And 1 back to zero
And you'll dilly-dally still
In the silliness of it all
Doing something, doing none
Finding a way to die, to grind

If only it were as easy as lying down
As a shut eye
As a sleep
Or better as a dream

So that's how you die Quraishiyah
Not of illness, not of oldness
Your stomach too fragile
To hold the glass of poison
You shoved down it

If you could have borne pain
Two wrists would have been slit

But you die still
Thinking of death
Too lazy to live
Too bored for another day

To the deep Quraishiyah
Like some great Pharaoh

Quraishiyah, the last of a punishable tribe
Who mocked some prophet
Harassed him so much
It's said that God himself had to
Write a chapter to set an example

Woe onto you, Quraishiyah
For eternity I presume
As all curses go

So wait for the sea to fold over you
That's a greater death
Than one that flew away
With the desert sands it was written on
Who remembers how Moses died!

24.

On sedentary wheels
Untiring passions
Rotate tirelessly
A wind blows away
My thoughts
Settles it
Blows it again

I flutter in emptiness
A speck floating away
That's how big I am
And my cotton mind
Smiles

Until the numbness
Inflamed with helpless fatality
Disintegrates in anger

An anger whose cause
Has long since
Been vacuumed
But still raspingly breathes
On its deathbed

Anger that boils down to nothing
Like when you have completed a 3917 pieces
Puzzle
And lost the last piece
Anger
Like when you've written 1543 pages
And your hard drive crashes
Anger
Like when you lose
A 100 bets one after the other
And play the 101st time
And lose

Anger so scalding
That it sizzles out instantly
Like burning embers under
A pail of water

A molten fiery ball
Of magma
That froths at the crater
Ready to spill out
In a vomiting burst of lava
But I pet it down
Till it whimpers
And lies down

A mirage materializes
And the ring turns blue

Rien ne va plus
Happiness creeps through
My indolent mind
And I bask in the joy of *oubli*

25.

Looping through the air
I stretch my wings
And soar
Through higher plains
And insane heights
I burst through the skies
And cotton candied clouds
Gluing to me like Velcro
I'm in heaven, I'm a bird
I'm an angel clothed
In fibrous white

I kick gravity and ride
Balls of water
At once visible and transparent
Shooting in and out
Of nothingness
Wrapped in more material
Than I carried
With buried feet

I'll fly so high
That I'll plummet in the sun

And burn myself
I was not dainty Icarus
Finicky fuss fuss
Ooh my wings! Oh wicked sun!

I hurtle on rocket like
Till the portrait was set right
And turned 180 degrees
Around
That f***ing gravity again
(Must show some respect to natural elements)
I speed up with battling hands
That I took for wings
Gathering speed
And busting through solid
Hurdles like they are nothing
But vapor
I whiz and zoom
Leaving behind light
At 200 miles per hour
Plunging
In no fortunate liquid

At the mouth of the precipice
I remembered
I tried to fly too
Well,
I won't be burned by the sun
Like that stupid Icarus
I'll just crash
Grounded in an unpalatable mash

Or who knows?
A delicious gravy
For some

26.

2 paths down the road
That's how long
Forever lasts
450 steps from your demise
And no more than 40 days
As prescribed by long-lasting
Scriptures

To forget is the remedy
And to forget we kneel
The pencil mistake on paper
Is more difficultly erased
Than grief palely scrolled
On the magic board of the mind

Folded in tear wraps
As other reeking garbage
Sadness, pain and other wastes
Are ejected from a body
Sane
And dissipate
As easy as
As normally as
As conveniently as

Hose down with a flush
Cause light
Is the natural state of humans

While someplace else
A lover for years carried his love
Under his arms
Slicing the face's off
Forgetfulness
To etch his looks
Eternal

Mona Lisa
In one eye hid an S
For Salai
In another eye an L
Was scratched to match
A Salai to Leonardo
Under the bridge of hell
72
Forever sealed a love beyond time
72?
It could mean everything
Or nothing
Or the addition of 2 names
84+42

To conquer eternity
I fished you out too
From the maelstrom
Of an anaesthetised mind

And made a collage
From scraps
Of memories

And there you stood
With tripods as legs
With one hand as long as a viper
And the other as short as a fang
Attached to the body of a fat cello
The colors were too thick to run over time
I was too
I chose Dali over Leonardo

27.

I have in my mouth
The taste of death
It has the saltness of the wide ocean
That flows on in cloudy wavelets
With a rocky dirty
Sandy beach
Stranded with corals
Where you take a walk with
Your shoes on
A far-off cry
Of a lost or half eaten
Quail
Carried by its fanged or
Nibbling predator
With a sallow water line
Where boulders lie
Hiding beneath them
Thousands of black
Urchins lurking with
Deadly quills
Ready to shoot them at
Itinerant feet or hands
Or puppy's mouth

Quill that kills
And I try to swallow
To remove the bitter after taste
Of a stale life

28.

Little footprints
Doggo's footprints
On the beach
I walk behind
Trying to gather a clue
About the dog
I am trailing
And I get bored
And I mess up the prints
With my large feet
Now the beach is full of me
Only
My treads, my marks,
My signature
And I wait for the tide to rise
To engulf me in its waters
But larger feet were more rapid
And engulfed me
In their markings

29.

In the clouds I see your face
All red and blue
In the form
Of an eclectus
With a big black shiny
Beak
That I yearn to pinch
Turning your head from
Right to left
Your skin as soft
As dew-covered
Woodland moss
And you look at me
With eyes
So tender
And blink
And I blink
And you blink back
Before being scattered
In a threaded mist
It then rained

30.

If only Artémise were here
My heart would have
Been beating still
And not just pumping
Away in my chest
I would smile still
And why not
Laugh at nothing
Now I'm just a puppet
Cut in timber, made of timber
And my wooden carved lips
Do not budge
Their congealed smile
Nor do my eyes glisten
Or moisten
Too fake to droop in sadness
Or to run
With tears

If only you were here
Artémise
You could have removed from my sheet
Heart

The grief paperweight
Cut in the form
Of a waxed cherub
Too sad to cry
Too sad to let it flow, drown away
Or to let it fly
To the wind
If you were here, the windows would have been opened
The curtains drawn away
And the sun greeted
And I would have drawn a breath
Instead of drawing a hole
In my heart

If only Artémise were here
The sea would not be only
Water
The mere half side of the world
Half soil, half water
Now there's nothing
To gaze at, or to gaze upon
Nothing to be taken by
Everything now makes
Perfect sense
And nothing left of
Wonder

And as you lay there
On the bottom
Of the ocean blue
With apathetic eyes

I lay here
In this cement box
Rotting quicker
Than you

31.

He was a cruel king
As loud-mouthed as evil
The spore of a bad blossom
Most certainly

And as I went a-by strolling
With an easy gait
It did not please the
All mighty king

What's that he cried
A whistling during my passage
I don't like your mien
What's that on your face
A smile I heard it is called
None of my subject can afford one

And he came up with
An idea to form and line me
With his other disciples
And to erase from my memory
Not only the meaning but the word
Happiness

Come to my kingdom
Come hither, come quickly
And bring me a gift
Wrapped in gold and silver

Gold and silver, I have nought
But two pennies and some nickels
In what should I wrap them
Your Majesty?
Asked I jestily

I could have demanded diamonds
Were I a monarch
Wicked and heartless
So, gold and silver
Only
If you please
Or I'll have naught
But your heart wrapped in tinfoil
Or why not
In newspaper

Of things that shine
I have only thirty-two
And they are in my mouth
The rest I'm afraid are all drab
And skin

But in the end he won the battle
Not for want of wit

On my side
Or for the excess of it on the other
The argument
Ran long enough
For his taste

In his magnanimity
He took nothing else
But a piece of my heart
A piece so little that
It was really nothing

Joyously live on, he said
And indeed I did
Deader than death
I go on
The shape of a smile cut out
In my heart

32.

He fed pigeons
With a hand
And created light
With the other
The mad scientist
In his dark tower
Mixed and brewed
In one pot
He threw in chemicals
And potions and deaths
And in another seeds
For his bird
His death ray towered
Besides his birdie's play gym
And while he worked on one
The pigeon did her workings on the other
Singing and talking
And always watching him
Upside down from the perch
Or at the rim of her bowl

The scientist must have been quite mad
It is said

He thought a pigeon was his friend
He thought a pigeon was his mate
And wife
A pigeon could comprehend
Said he
And read lines
That need not be uttered
Or decipher
Emotions hidden
He was berserk
He must have been
Or else it was the world that was so
Who did not understand the
Lingo of the beak

"Yes, I loved that pigeon
I loved her
As a man loves a woman
And she loved me
When she was ill, I knew
And understood
She came to my room and
I stayed besides her
For days
I nursed her back
To health
That pigeon was the joy
Of my life
If she needed me,
Nothing else mattered
As long as I had her

There was purpose
In my life"

And light came out of his fingers
And he brewed and mixed
Rocks told him their secrets
And the constellations
Spoke to him in
Hieroglyphs
He could add and multiply
The emptiness of space
That fills the universe
He could minus matter
And divide energy
And draw magic
With a chalk

He chanted incantations
Drew plans
He invented so many machines they say
The sorcerer's baton
Or broom
Seemed quite useless
When compared to his abracadabrian
Machinations

He conjured
Equations and conjunctions
And neither the farthest
Planet
Nor the sun

Could he not fathom
By his calculations

And yet, said they, quite mad
N'est-ce pas ?
Since with a pigeon he shared
Secrets and desires
And dreamt
Of fantasies
If only one had wings
Or the other hands
But still they thrived on
Together
Since to a pigeon he conversed
And the pigeon talked back to him
Since his love was a love that
Knew nothing of species
Of birds and humans

"But there was a pigeon
A beautiful bird
Pure white with light gray tips
On its wing
That one was different
I would know that pigeon anywhere"

And their love grew
Human and pigeon
The whole sky was
At Pigeon's feet
But she still chose

To return to the
Claustrophobic apartment
Of her lover
He was bird
She was human
Or vice versa
It mattered none
What garb they were in

"Then one night
As I was lying in my bed in the dark
Solving problems
As usual
She flew in through the open window and stood on my desk
I knew she wanted me
She wanted to tell me something
Important
So I got up and went to her
As I looked at her
I knew she wanted to tell me
She was dying

And then, as I got her message
There came a light from her eyes —
Powerful beams of light
Yes, it was a real light
A powerful
Dazzling, blinding light,
A light more intense than
I had ever produced
By the most powerful lamps in my laboratory."

He generated lightnings
Blind light with special glasses
But they were dull
To the light
Of his passing
Beloved eyes
He held her little body
In his short-circuited
Fingers
And wished he had enough
Electricity
To burn down the world
And blow it away into a fistful
Of ash

"When that pigeon died,
Something went out of my life
Up to that time
I knew with a certainty
That I would complete my work
No matter how ambitious my program
But when that something went
Out of my life
I knew my life's work
Was finished."

He had electric fingers
And yet. . .
He could build a death ray
Wipe out humanity

And yet. . .
Could not build a contraption
To bring back
The love of his life

But he was the lightman
And his love as light
Lightly followed his
Every step
Where he thought
Obscurity now resided
Light found a way
And in a dream
A yellow light
A beam that once announced death
Uttered
I'm so good where I am now

33.

Amor Fati
Tell that to the mother
Who backed on her little boy
In the garage
Tell the father
Who let the stove on
For too long
And the little swaddling
Baby girl that had
The boiling water fell on her
To love his destiny
Do tell the grandmother
Who was talking to her
Long met friend
While her grandchild
Fell in the pool
To love her fate
Do tell
The drunken driver
Crashing in the family car
That it was his destiny
At fault and he could accept it
Nevertheless

He'll sure embrace
This philosophy
But pray do tell
That to the family of five
Inside the car
That is now only
A family of one
Amor fati

No, what does not kill me
Does not make me
Stronger
It only makes me
Not dead
Left
And tolerable
Of whatever would fall
Next
It does not
Make me resilient
It just makes everything
Paler in comparison
It makes me indifferent
Bring your flood now,
Bring your pests
And storms
Bring wars
Or diseases
Death is only an event
When you think about it
People have been dying

Again
And all over
And it never ends

No, I'm not stronger
I just have nothing
Going on
That seems better
Than death

34.

It grew darker
And heavier
But it still did not rain
For days and weeks
And months
Not a drop of water shed
And though the
Hearty cloud blew like a
Ripe balloon
It refused to pop
Barren and parched
Eyes look to the sky
For an ounce of pity
And dried up hands
Cup in withered longing
A shrill sound escapes
My wrinkled lips
An extinguished thunder
That whimpers pathetically
But still my eyes remain glassy
Sorrow drowns my heart
While my waterproof eyes
Do not leak

I try to pour out the hurt
To let flow the pain
But it all just fills up
Against the dam of my chest
And finds no way
Out
No bursting
No spilling
But somehow
Finds the place
To keep
Filling

35.

Blood spilling
Guts wrenching and crying out
In the end, God's name
Bowels, intestines,
And all matters inside
Now shamelessly lying outside
Bodies that once were
Still are, but only
Shredded, decorticated
And bled
And God is there
All right
Throning above it all
With a satisfied smile
And an approving nod
The yells did not reach his ears
Good for Him
And the sight
Did not rebuke his appetite
Either
Just was His middle name
Afterall
I remained in front of the tableau for hours

That's the middle place
I heard
And wondered what hell was like
God still uses such archaic
Methods of torture
What's with all the cutting, and tearing
It would seem He was making a salad
Out there
What's with the axes, and knives,
And ropes, and picks
When there are injections and electrocutions
For a cleaner job
That's why heaven is so archaic too
Only gardens and fountains
And prairies and trees
God, would I miss my iPad!

36.

Message to Yo-Yo Ma

A sound that elevates
That compels your spirit
To soar high and above
To rise to the heavens
And to feel the power of elation
But also a sound that
Puts you down
Crushes your spirit
Under its boots
And kicks you in the guts
And you can't take it anymore
But it goes in crescendo
And kicks you again
A music that creates
A warmth in your heart
And renders everything beautiful
And creates a little heaven
In your sleeping mind
But at the same time
A music that fells you
On your knees

Strikes you at your lowest
And rips your chest
And lets it bleed
That's Bach cello
Suite for you

37.

I'm a castle
An old one
Covered in vines
And impenetrable thorns
I'm a castle
Made of rocks
And curses
Of a thousand years
I'm a castle standing
On the verge of a precipice
Losing a few pebbles
But still erect
I'm a castle
With towers that stretch
To the sky
And floundering foundations
I am a castle
With ceilings
Filled with cobwebs
And cockroaches matting the floors
And living up my sleeves
I am cursed to be
On the brink of collapsing

I stagger in place
And like the forlorn mountain
In the distance
I count the years
Gone by and those yet to come
And my turrets blink helplessly
At the passing sun
While my wall weeps
Its emptiness

38.

A little yellow bird
Visits me from heaven
A blue-green bird
As bright and orange as the sun
Gleaming golden
In the drabness of my doorstep
And she nonchalantly perches on the white handle
Two frail pink twigs
With tiny black claws gleaming
Against the chalky aluminium
Of my door
And she knocks
With flaming red beak
Then she waits on my green threshold
On the mat dirty and brownish
With wiped soles
The little bird from heaven is not as any bird
As I've ever seen
It shines in daylight
And threatens to burn errant fingers
That come too near
And I wonder why it chose my door
Neither marked nor special

Just another boring
Insignificant frame
While up it flies again
Up to the handle
And knocks again
And I stand on the other side of the door
Blandly procrastinating
Whether I should open that door
Or not
She knocks twice more
While stunned with indecisiveness
I ask what if she flies away
When I open the door
And she flies away
A yellow dot
In a pale blue sky
Where a bigger red disk of molten red
Drowns the clouds around it
In a carmine aura

39.

There'll be sure signs of the apocalypse
They say
Mountains will float around
As cotton
The sea will bubble and boil
Animals will talk
The sun will turn water
And the sky ripped in
Two
But
Nobody told me
Nobody told me you'll be gone
Days crept on, the sky smiled on
The sun burnt on
The earth will be torn
The prophet will come back
Or go back
Nobody can keep tracks of his coming
And going anymore
And Alexander himself spewed
From his grave
But nobody made a sign
No wave, no nod

Before you were gone
The ground kept stable
The seers kept sinning
And praying
And eat on the forbidden lamb
Promised to heaven
And I went on normally
Ignoring you
Because there should have been
Tomorrow
We lived our parallel journey
Once again
Once last
And I told you good night
À demain

40.

I stabbed once
And first went the anger
And I stabbed twice
There flew the hate
I stabbed thrice
And there went the love

Anna Maria stood in front of the corpse
Wondering what brought her there
It was like being
In front of a Monteverdi
Or a Michael Angelo
Something ripped inside her
The gut-wrenching hate
Was pulled out of her
Like a threaded intestine
And she stood now empty
While her emotions evaporated
Into oblivion

Leaving place to a sole feeling
A lasting impression
Of déjà-vu

She remembered
Every thrust
Every drop of blood that squirted
On her face
And yet, this never happened
Before

It was both premonition
And
Memory

Anna Maria stood with this
Dagger
On her birth bed
And she travelled back
And she travelled forth
She killed before
And after
And held the dagger
On her death bed

A ripple
Travels back
And forth
On the timeline
And echoes
In a loop
Indefinitely chastising
Anna Maria

41.

You now live behind the cloud
Of my mind
A blur
Is all that remains
You are not
You are nowhere
Not even in my dreams
A blank
A space between
2 words
I thought I'll reach you
But every time I extend my hand
It returns empty
Remembrances
Moments engraved
All washes away
While I go on
Every day now
Only a day without you
And life runs long
And whether castles, or forests,
Or worlds
All fall in silent ruins

While
False images, false memories,
Now weave through my mind
Only your name keeps coming true to me
Because I still use it as
Password

42.

Blood drops are falling from my hand
And just like the boiling water that kills all the squid
I burn in my bath
Those blood drops are falling from my hand, they keep falling

So the sun burns out, and God has walked the plank
I decided what the heck, since life is just a blank
A wheel with no end
Those blood drops are falling from my hand, they keep falling

Crush you under its feet
Breaks you like a candlestick
But keeps you here, keeps on going
And it laughs cause that is life schtick

Blood drops keep falling from my hand
And they say I am too dark, people need to be cheered
Give them some sugar
They want to believe the poor creepers in the sewer that
Brushing feces
Is better than dying

And the silver lining is just beneath the pile of dung

43.

Imagine if we never really
Die
And the afterlife
Is nothing
But a long slumber

A dead heart
Under 6 piles of dirt
With an alive brain
That thinks on
That feels on

Aware of an eyeball being gnawed
Or something slithering in your vagina
An alive thing
Hanging by itself
And that do not need a body
To thrust a way inside

Imagine breathing the dark
Growing in the dark
Casted in the womb
Of a granular red earth

Knowing supper time
Now means you are the feast

They imagined heaven
And hell
And torture is the worst they
Could think of
Object still
Bloody still
And moving still

But what if
Hell is just you
Lying there
With an alive brain
Pumping still
Till eternity
Or eternally

44.

Ho Ho Ho
I come in good tidings to
Share the cheers
Ho Ho Ho

We need comic relief
In all these tragedies
Come on, give us a happy line
We don't have hope enough

We paint out faces white
Our hearts black
And pout not
Behind backs

It's a new world
The camera that once caught souvenirs
Now catches faked elation
To be shared

And still life is sad
And they need cheer
This is too dark

Can't read it,
Need our spirit lifted
Like all the other parts
Of our malfunctioning body

Ho Ho Ho
We want happy endings
A merry here
A joy there
To make it all palatable
Otherwise we lose interest

We can't look at bleakness for too long
Our minds are too sealed for that
We want air in the face,
Feet in the sands
And summer on our skins
And even if this has been written a thousand times
We will copy it a thousand times more
With our stupidly plastered smile
Ho Ho Ho

And Ho Ho Ho
I say to them
I don't write to give cheer
Peel off your face,
Gouge out your eyes and drive a stake through your heart
In front of no mirror
And then you'll get it

It's in Dostoyevsky's basement
It's in Kafka's court
And it's in Loujine's head

And if you find it
Share the cheer
Ho Ho Ho

45.

I dreamt for my dad
A watery grave
Blue in the bottom
And blue on top
With dark obsidian corals
And bleeding sands
Swinging for eternity
Or until resurrection
Cradled in the warm embrace
Of foamy waves
And sea turtles
Lying in a dream
With fishes green,
Blue and orange
Flying about his eternal bedside
Hum a song
That only mermaids could understand
And he in his canopy
Wishing but not believing
For a heaven
More heavenly than this sepulcher

With this happy image
I dug on
Never tiring
Never stopping
Wide enough
Deep enough

And called my father
And I kicked my father
In the grave
And waited for it
To rain

46.

It was that time again
To lay my head
On the bare pillow
And the naked mattress
One yellowed with tears
And drools
The other soiled with perspiration
I throw my dead body
And close my eyes
To unsee the barrenness
The dolls and toys
And I tighten my fingers
Around your *doudou*
To go through
This ritual
I now sleep at the sound of the
Rising sun
And wake up
With the setting
Calls of the birds

47.

They say the sun rise
Is the most beautiful thing
Alas, they do not see
A burning star
But
The imagery
The metaphor
To guile their dormant mind
New day
New page
New hope
Wow still and wow again

Real beauty
Lies in the eyes
It is
Before
Before the sunrise
When the sky
And the clouds
Are drenched in red
Bleeding
Bleeding to create something new

Or bleeding because
It never ends
Because however they try
To smother that stupid sun
However cut and bruised
And bloody
He wakes up again and goes about
His little tedious
Routinely unworthy business
And every day before lighting the world
The paths of others
As a private joke
He bathes all
Everyone and everything
In his drowning blood

Still
Blind and deaf
They chose the sun
After he has shed
His bloody skin
To bathe in his
Glorious orange glow

48.

Why do I feel
Everything lived
Has been lived before
The turmoil
That wrecks me
Belongs to a new sadness
And yet
I know and recall
Having felt the same
Years before
For a regrettable whimsy
The same dejection
The same tears
The same hopelessness
I've never been in such pain
Before
And yet
I remember feeling same
For a day that ran too long
For a summer too moist
And for a lost watch
I am wracked with false and shallow emotions
Repetitive as the sun

Insipid as another day
Carrying deep momentarily meaning
In the span of a tear drop

49.

I wish to tear down
The sky
To find you behind
If only my hands
Could reach up
And burn its fragile fabric
I wish everything
And everyone
Were ugly
And dejected
That the world should burn down
Or drown
Where are the gods
And where are the calamities
When you need one
Destroy every ounce of beauty
In every nook
Of this pestilential earth
Words like
Beautiful and joy
Erased
If only desolation was not
Just a promise

And if this may not be so
I wish to be blinded
And deafened
So my eyes would see no more than
The darkness of my heart
And my ears would hear nothing more than
The bleakness of my mind
And I'll pass through life
Stealthily
Without a sound, without neither thumb
Nor foot print
Of my existence

50.

A forlorn orange
Leaflike bird
Fell from the sky
Into my hands
Like an autumn leaf
That could hang
No more
On the almost naked branch
It had been holding on to
For life
A breathing living leaf
An orange chick
Fit for a palm
Chirping and blinking
Life
That bleaches away
And orange wings
Turned brown
Turned drab
And I put it
Between immortal lines
But still
The pages ate through it

And left a moth holed
Relic
That decayed through my fingers
Leaving my bare arm
A wintery naked bark

www.ingramcontent.com/pod-product-compliance
Lightning Source LLC
Chambersburg PA
CBHW070827100426
42813CB00003B/517